Simple and Delicious

Certified Nutritionist, Kae Izena's

okinawa
soup
RecipeBook

Soups are the solo acts which take center stage on our dining table.

The source for happiness hides
within a delightfully tasty and inspiring meal.

contents

- 10 Opening Interview with Kae Izena
- 12 Basic Japanese Cooking Techniques
- 18 Okinawa's Island Pride Vegetables

22 Spring Soup Recipes

- 24 Nsunaba Pottage
- 26 Okinawan Carrot Soup with Brown Rice
- 28 Spring Cabbage and Okinawan Leek Pottage
- 30 Fresh Sweet Corn Pottage
- 32 Asa Soup
- 34 Cream of Paprika
- 36 Muji Soup
- 38 Cream of Soy with Tofu

40 "Soup" - The Secret All-Around Ingredient

42 Summer Soup Recipes

- 44 Okura Soup
- 46 Togan Soup
- 48 Nakami Soup
- 50 Chilled Peach Pottage
- 52 Exotic Okinawa
- 54 Chilled Watermelon and Kiwi Fruit Soup
- 56 Asian Flavored Sparassis (Cauliflower Mushroom) Soup

58 In Search for "The Chosen" Ingredient: Seafood Episode

60 Autumn Soup Recipes

- 62 Chinnuku Pottage
- 64 Cream of Okinawan Pumpkin
- 66 Okinawan Burdock Soup
- 68 Cream of Mushroom and Ginger
- 70 Cream of Malabar Spinach
- 72 Beni Imo (Purple Yam) and Chestnut Soup
- 74 Beni Imo and Okinawan Vegetable Soup
- 76 Kandaba Pottage
- 78 Japanese Whole Fish Soup

80 In Search for "The Chosen" Ingredient: Vegetable Episode

84 Winter Soup Recipes

- 86 Winter Okinawan Vegetable and Beef Soup
- 88 Spicy Yushi Dofu and Garlic Leaves Soup
- 90 Chopped Billfish and Vegetable Soup
- 92 Cream of Okinawan Carrot
- 94 Tender Okinawan Vegetables Soup
- 96 Inamu duchi
- 98 Cream of Chinese Cabbage and Scallops

- 100 Introduction to the KAE Project
- 102 Student Testimonials

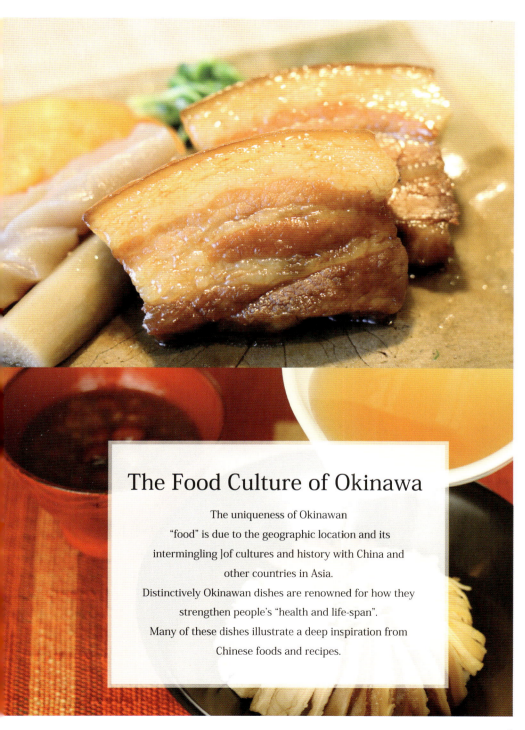

The Food Culture of Okinawa

The uniqueness of Okinawan "food" is due to the geographic location and its intermingling]of cultures and history with China and other countries in Asia.
Distinctively Okinawan dishes are renowned for how they strengthen people's "health and life-span".
Many of these dishes illustrate a deep inspiration from Chinese foods and recipes.

An Interview with
Kae Izena

My wish: To restore Okinawa as the 'Island with the Longest-Lived People" with recipes for vegetable filled Soup

For those Kae Izena fans, this 3rd book consists of easy to prepare and nutritious "soups" for you! Enjoy!

A single bowl of soup can become the main dish for a meal.

The story in creating this book begins with my wish to regain Okinawa's standing as the "Island of Long Life". I wanted to create a recipe book which would draw the interest of the younger and new generation of Okinawa. My hope was that the ease in preparation, the nutritional value, and taste of each recipe would persuade them to pick up the book. It dawned on me on the best way was in the form of soups. Soups can be very convenient and all-purpose dish. It can be eaten when you don't have an appetite, when you want to store and save portions for the future, and be made to be a main dish or side dish. Cooking in general can feel like a hassle. "The soup" can help relieve this pressure while assuring you are taking in enough nutrients for your body. Let's enjoy cooking without the pressure.

The new challenge: "Regain Okinawa's standing as the "Island with the Longest-Lived People".

Okinawa used to be the "Island with the Longest-Lived People". However, this reputation is at a brink of danger of being lost. The change in diet, lifestyle, and societal environment has greatly changed and put this reputation at risk. I have advocated various movements in raising the awareness of the role of "food". Food is the foundation of our health. Unfortunately, things have not moved in a positive direction. I have realized that there are limits to my activities and efforts. Therefore, I am reaching out to individuals in various fields related to "food" so that we can create the "Team Ganju". The aim of "Team Ganju" is to deepen the understanding and consciousness toward agriculture and its production through hands-on experience. We take participants to see, feel, and think about the food in Okinawa. There is also a special training group of 10 individuals who work alongside myself to brainstorm ways on how to progress the team's aims. This last spring, our studio moved from Shuri to Yomitan city. In our new home, we focus on providing hands-on experience in crop growing, training seminars, and other activities which deepen the relationships between the grower and consumer.

The source for happiness lies in the quality of a meal.

Food truly makes me happy. I will never be able to remove it from the list of things that make me happy. Regardless of how much time and effort it takes, people find ways to stay happy. The only difference is that I fuel my compassion with "food". How about you? Whether it is leisure, sports, work, or the path of success they had chosen, I wish people will continue to cherish those things that bring them happiness and believe in their ideals.

<Kae Izena's Profile>
Hometown:Okinawa Prefecture, Naha city
1991 Est. "Kae Health Planning"
2015 Director of Operations for the Total Wellness Project 2016 Operations transferred to Yomitan. Rebranded "Kae Project". Kae Project offers professional health and beauty services, advising on nutrient and exercising, and houses a cooking school. "We are what we eat", is her motto and actively reaches out through various television, radio, and newspaper media outlets. She shares her secrets of how to polish up peoples beauty through changing their mindset toward dieting and healthy cooking.

Basic Japanese Cooking Techniques

How ingredients are cut and prepared make a big difference in the final taste and enjoyment of each dish.In the next chapter, we introduce some Basic Japanese Cooking Techniques so you can fully enjoy each recipe.

Knife Techniques

Take a look at some common knife techniques for specific ingredients and Japanese recipes.

● Favorable ingredient   ● Favorable dish or recipe

Knife Technique 1 | Thick Circular Slices (Wa-giri)

Each cut should be identical (width) and portions should be circular in shape.

- ● Japanese radishes (daikon), carrots, various potatoes and yams, eggplants (aubergines)
- ● stews, frying

Knife Technique 2 | The Ginkgo Leaf (Ichou-giri)

Portions should be cut to form shapes like that of the Ginkgo Leaf (a circle cut into quarters). The width will vary based on the recipe.

- ● daikons, carrots, various potatoes and yams
- ● sauté, stews, soups, pickling

Knife Technique 3 | Wedges (Ran-giri)

Cut ingredients into wedges by rotating and cutting it at various angles. Each cut surface should vary in shape.

- ● daikons, carrots, burdocks, cucumbers
- ● stews, soups

Knife Technique 4 | Thin Round Slices (Koguchi-giri)

Begin at the point of the ingredient and cut into thin slices. Tuck in knuckles and use the edge of your finger as a guide to cut.

- ● cucumbers, leeks
- ● Sumono (vinegared side dishes), Aemono (dressed side dish), salads, condiments

Knife Technique 5 | Thin Rectangular Strips (Tanzaku-giri)

Cut to preferred length. Then cut along fibers to make even sized rectangular strips.

- ● daikons, carrots, cucumbers
- ● soups, dressed side dish, vinegared side dishes

Knife Technique 6 | Rectangular Bars (Yuzuki-giri)

First cut ingredients to the preferred length. Then cut into 1 cm by 1 cm rectangular bars.

- ● daikons, carrots, cucumbers
- ● soups, dressed side dish, vinegared side dishes, pickling

Knife Techniques

● Favorable ingredient ● Favorable dish or recipe

Knife Technique 7 | Edging (Men-dori)

Trim edges of thick vegetables slices to maintain the shape of it when cooked. Larger surface area allows for more flavor to seep in.

● daikons, various potatoes and yams, squash and pumpkins
● stews

Knife Technique 8 | Hidden Slits (Kakushi-bouchou)

Cut two slits which extend from each edge on the circular surface of the ingredient. Slits should be and half the thickness deep to allow flavor to seep in and making eating easier.

● daikon ● stews

Knife Technique 9 | Random Shaped Wedges (Zaku-giri)

Chop leaf vegetables into portions larger than bite size. "Zaku" is said to be the sound the leaf make when chopping it.

● cabbages, spinach, Chinese cabbages
● sauté, stew, soups

Knife Technique 10 | Bite Sizes (Hitokuchi-dai)

Cut ingredients in bite size portions. The shape of the portions can be altered based on the ingredient (e.g. wedges, random).

● daikon, carrots, various potatoes and yams
● stews

Knife Technique 11 | Julienne-Cucumber (Kyuri-no-sen-giri)

For Chinese Dishes: Cut to preferred length, then stack slice into evenly sized strips.

For Japanese Dishes: Cut into slices, then cut at angle into strips.

Recommended for Chinese dishes   Recommended for Japanese dishes

RIGHT Image: Japanese dishes emphasizes color. Cut so skin remains on the tips of the strips.

LEFT Image: Chinese dishes emphasizes uniformity: Cut so each strip is the same length and color.

Food Storing Techniques

How to Pickle Ingredients

Directions

①.Combine vinegar and sugar (ratio of vinegar to sugar is 2:1) to make the pickling liquid.
②.Cut preferred vegetables and place in well disinfected (boiled in hot water) jar.
③. Combine ingredients from Step 1 to Step 2 until all the ingredients are immersed in the liquid.
※Hijiki (fine pre-dried seaweed) can be pickled in the liquid without it being rehydrated.
※Pickles can be stored for 1 to 2 months in the refrigerator.
Ingredients
Your favorite pickled ingredient … Amount is as preferred
Vinegar … Amount based on ingredients being pickled   Sugar … Half of amount of vinegar

How to make Togan (Okinawan Melons) Cubes

Place the Togan so that it may be secured firmly and remove the skin.

Firmly hold the Togan diagonally and grate.

Pour Togan evenly in an ice tray.

How to make Dry Peucedanum (a.k.a. Sakuna) Leaves.

Remove the leaves of the peucedanum from stems by cutting along the edges connecting each leaf together.

Dry out leaves by heating it in the microwave.

Place dry peucedanum leaves in a plastic bag, break up gently in small pieces.

Measuring Techniques

A precise measurement allows for a precise taste!

Basic Measuring Tools, Utensils, and Scales for Cooking

Make sure you have measuring cups and spoons in hand. When measuring with a measuring cup, remember that 1 cup equals 200 ml. When measuring with a measuring spoon, remember that 1 table spoon equals 15 ml and 1 teaspoon equals 5 ml.

"1 GO and 1 CUP are NOT the same amount."

The measurement for rice is "GO = 180 ml". This is not equal to 1 cup (200ml).

Weighing or Measuring Various Dry Ingredients

1 Table Spoon

Scoop up dry ingredients with a spoon. Scrape surface flat to remove excess.

½ Table Spoon

Repeat steps to measure 1 table spoon. Then, use the wooden spatula to scrape half the amount from the spoon.

¼ Table Spoon

Halve the 1/2 Table Spoon with wooden spatula.

Weighing or Measuring Various Liquids

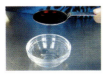

1 Table Spoon

Scoop enough to fill the entire spoon up to the brim.

½ Table Spoon

Scoop enough to fill 2/3 of the spoon.

Weighing or Measuring by Hand

A Pinch

Pinch with pointer, middle, and thumb. Amount roughly equal to 1/2 a teaspoon.

A Sprinkle or A Little

Pinch with point and thumb. Amount roughly equal to 1/4 of a teaspoon.

Reference for the Weighing Ingredients by Hand

Reference for Weighing Ingredients by Hand: A handful is roughly 100 g. Slices held on top of the pointer, middle, and ring finger is roughly 70-80 g. Japanese L/M-size eggs are roughly 60/50 g each.

Reference for how much is a Piece of Ginger or Garlic

A piece of ginger refers to roughly 2 cm which is almost equal to size of the thumb. A single clove of garlic is roughly 10 g.

Parboiling and Boiling Techniques

The secret technique of parboiling and boiling.

Parboiling or Boiling from water at room temperature

Use for root vegetables or things grown underground (e.g. potatoes, yams, daikon, radishes).

Parboiling or Boiling in water at boiling temperature

Use for green-colored vegetables (e.g. spinach). Water should be boiling prior to placing ingredients inside.

Tips for Parboiling or Boiling

Add salt to the water
This is best to maintain and brighten the color of green vegetables.

Add vinegar to the water
This is best for Renkon (lotus root) and cauliflowers.

Use the remaining water from rinsing rice
This is best for parboiling daikon (radishes) and takenoko (bamboo shoots).

After Ingredients have been Parboiled or Boiled

Placing ingredients in ice cold water

To maintain or brighten the color of ingredients such as spinach and other green vegetables which are acidic or lose its color once heated, should be soaked in ice cold water immediately.

Placing ingredients in a sieve or strainer

Use instruments to maintain aroma of vegetables (bean sprouts, broccolis, cauliflowers). Utilize self-cooking technique by removing ingredients before they are fully boiled in the instruments (i.e. thick cut vegetables).

Preparing ingredients using a microwave

Place ingredients in heat-resistant containers and splash it with water. This is a more convenient and easier method to get the job done than using a pot or pan.

How to parboil or boil shelled fish (e.g. clams)

Long-neck Clams should be boiled from water at room temperature

Place in water before boiling point to fully cook properly

Short-necked Clams should be boiled in water at boiling temperature

Cooks quickly and the broth from the clam can be used to add Umami to other recipes.

Okinawa's Island Pride Vegetables
shima yasai
The more you know, the better it tastes!

Okinawa is blessed with extended sunshine and is a treasure chest of nutritious vegetables. During each vegetable's season, their price becomes quite affordable so people can line their dinner table with them.

Chinkuwa
(Okinawan Squash)

Rich in Vitamin A. Recommended for soups because it is full of water and also great with vegetable sauté. Choose one with dark skin and solid in weight.

Season: June to October

Chidekuni
(Okinawan Carrot)

Rich in Caroten and to absorb as much as you can, cook it in oil. Chidekuni means "Yellow Carrot" in the Ryukyuan dialect. There is an old traditional practice to help the body fight a cold by eating yellow carrots and pork liver stew (Chimushinji).

Season: November to February

Papaya
(A vegetable version of the Papaya)

Rich in Vitamin C and the meat of the vegetable is often used in stir fries. It also contains the nutrient, Papain, which can be taken in by the body through salads or it wrapped in slices of ham. There are many other ways to prepare the vegetable such as stews, pickles, and dried. It's a handy ingredient to have and the texture is not lost even if stored in the refrigerator.

Season: July to September

Sakuna (Peucedanum Flower)

Rich in Vitamin C and Calcium. There is an old saying that it is good for soar throats (coughing). It's distinct bitterness is also used to remove the meaty smell from goat stew. The soft leaves can be used for Aemon (dressed side dishes). It can also be dried to use add a sharp taste to your soups.

Season: All Year

Nsunaba (Swiss chard)

Rich in vitamins, folic acids, iron, and dietary fibers. Big leaves with thick meaty stems. It possesses a distinct bitterness if eaten raw, so don't forget to parboil it before cooking it. You can enjoy it in vinegar Miso dressed side-dishes, stir fries, and other tasty dishes.

Season: January to April

Okinawan Rakyo
(Islander Leek)

Consists of the chemical Adenosine, which helps lower the risk of blood clotting. Recipes include, sautéing, pickling, dressed side dishes, and even can be made into paste to be stored for long periods of time. In stores between early Spring through the beginning of the Summer.

Season: March to June

Gunbo
(Okinawan Burdock)

Rich in dietary fibers and calium. When in season, its skin is relatively soft and as part of preparing it to be cooked, you can use an aluminum sponge to brush the skin off. The Okinawan burdock is often seen in Tonjiru (pork and vegetable soup), Kinpira Gobou (sweet julienne burdock), and in stews. It can also be enjoyed by simply taking thin ones and grilling them.

Season: All Year

Goya (Bitter Gourd)

Contains a type of Vitamin C which does not easily breakdown when cooked and tastes great when cooked with oils. The bitter taste comes from the chemical, Momordicin, which helps strengthen your digestive system and stimulate your appetite. It is an ingredient well fitted for when the Summer heat begins draining you of your energy.

Season: April to September

Kandaba
(Edible Arrowroot)

Rich in Vitamin A, C, B1, B2, and also polyphenol and dietary fibers. Unlike the leaves of the yam, it is an edible leaf vegetable. It is definitely a vegetable more people should try to add to their diet.

Season: June to November

Ninniku-ha
(Garlic Leaves)

Rich in calcium, various vitamins, iron, and its spicy tastes is caused by the chemical Iline. Look for the one with the tenderest leaves, but remember that it can go bad quickly so try to use it in dishes as soon as you can.

Season: December to February

Unche
(Water Spinach)

It is a Summer vegetable that is rich in various vitamins, calcium, carotene, and iron. The stems are relatively soft and have a distinctive texture. The entire vegetable is edible (sections near the roots, too). Generally used in stir fry dishes, but also used in dressed side dishes and pickled dishes.

Season: May to September

Okinawa's Island Pride Vegetables
島やさい
shima yasai
The more you know, the better it tastes!

Tamuji
(Mountain yam stems)

Rich in dietary fibers, calcium, and calium. To remove bitterness, cut along the fibers and soak in water. In Okinawa it is used in traditional events and festivals. You can often see it in dishes such as Muji jiru (pork and yam soup), and Douruwakashi (yam, pork, vegetable, and fish paste).

Season: November to February

Nmo
(Okinawan Purple Yams)

Richi in starch, various vitamins, calium, calcium, and dietary fibers. It possesses a sweet taste and soft texture. There are various ways to prepare the Nmo such as purple yam rice, grilled yam, tempura, and various snack recipes.

Season: August to January

Hamana
(New Zealand Spinach)

This ingredient grows on the shores and beaches of the island. It contains Oxalic acids so make sure to parboil before cooking. It can be prepared in dishes such as dressed side dishes, miso soup, and stir fry.

Season: May to October

Islander Shoga
(Ginger)

The chemicals such as Gingerol and Shogaol helps to increase blood circulation in the body for those people who have trouble keeping their body warm. You can feel how it really "warms-up" the body in the winter with dishes such as Ginger tea, soups, and stir fries. It can also be pickled in vinegar to be stored for long periods of time.

Season: December to May

Bijyun
(Malabar spinach)

Rich in Beta Carotene, calcium, magnesium, iron, and Vitamin C. It is one of the vegetables rich in various nutrients. It can be enjoyed by boiling, sautéing, and in soups.

Season: June to October

Njana
(Scientific Name: Ixeris dentate
<Recipes reference are to the leaves>)

Rich in carotene and calcium. Has a distinctly strong bitterness, but if properly removed, there are wide array of recipes in which it can be used in. Traditionally it has been used in Squid-ink soup however, it is also used in sautés, dressed side dishes, tempura, and porridges.

Season: December to May

Jibui
(Okinawan Melon)

The Jibui is made up of 96% water, rich in Vitamin C, and low in calories. It is fit for stews and soups. It especially tasty with Okinawan Pork ribs (Soki soup). When choosing the right one, I recommend the bigger ones versus the smaller ones. To make storing easier and leave for future use, cut the remaining portion of the Jibui, grate it down to small portions, and place it in the freezer.

Season: April to September

Asa (Okinawan Kelp)

The Asa is made up of 40% dietary fibers and is rich in calcium, Vitamin A, and Folic acids. Recipes include and not limited to, soups, stems, and various dishes with eggs.
Season: January to March

Chinnuku
(Mountain Yam)

Rich in carbohydrates, Vitamin B1, dietary fibers, and calium. It is often used in the traditional Okinawan dish "Jushi" (rice cooked together with the yam). Other recipes include stews, soups, gratins, and stir fries.
Season: All year

Okinawan Ninjin (Carrot)

The bright orange is a sign that it is rich in carotene and once absorbed by the body turns into Vitamin A. Ingredients with Carotene taste great and is better absorbed when cooked with oil. A traditional Okinawan dish it is often used in is "Ninjinn Shirishiri" (sautéd julienne carrots with eggs). It can also be prepared in stews and stir fries, too.

Season: December to March

Nasutachiumu
(Nasturtium or Species of Indian cress)

Rich in Vitamin C and iron. The leaves also can act as a disinfectant. It has a spicy aroma, and the parts of the ingredients can be used in various ways. For example, the flowers are often used in salads, leaves in sandwiches, and the buds can be pickled. Edible flowers such as this can help both brightening up your dish and also help make it healthier.

Season: April to June

Spring Soup Recipes
Delicious spring soup

A new beginning, a new journey.
For some, this season marks a new adventure in a new place.
I hope this season brings everybody the excitement of each
new day and the sparkle of each new encounter.
It is also a season fill your body and soul with various nutrients.
I hope each soup is a reassurance
to start a new chapter in your life.

Spring Soup Recipes

1 Nsunaba Pottage

2 Okinawan Carrot Soup with Brown Rice

3 Spring Cabbage and Okinawan Leek Pottage

4 Fresh Sweet Corn Pottage

5 Asa Soup

6 Cream of Paprika

7 Muji Soup

8 Cream of Soy with Tōfu

Spring Soup

A Homage to Okinawan Vegetables

SPRING SOUP RECIPE

Nsunaba Pottage Soup

Cooking time 20minutes 【121kcal (Dairy milk)・106kcal・82kcal (Almond milk)・Per serving】
(※Cooling time not included.)

kae's voice

It takes time to properly cook recipes which involve stewing. But, I often use that time to enjoy daydreaming about different things. It is a special time for me that I love.

Ingredients (Yield: 4 servings)

Nsunabā (Swiss Chard) ··· 1bunch (100g)
Onion ·························· 1/2 onion
⎡ Chicken Consommé ········· 1 package
Ⓐ Water ·························· 200cc
⎣ Rice ···························· 60g
Dairy milk ····················· 300cc
Salt ···························· to taste
Pepper ·························· to taste
Oil ····························· 1 tablespoon

Directions

❶ Separate the leaves and stems of the Nsunaba, wash both with water, and remove the excess water with a strainer. Chop leaves into 2-3 cm sizes and stems into 2 cm pieces. Cut onions into julienne strips.

❷ Warm oil in a pot and sauté the onions until they are light brown color. Add Nsunaba and lightly sauté the ingredients.

❸ Add the pre-made mixture Ⓐ to the content made in Step ❷ and heat to boil. Once it begins to boil, cover the pot and allow it to simmer on low heat for 5 minutes. Turn off heat once it has simmered, add milk (dairy), and allow it to cool. Once cooled, place it in a blender to blend.

❹ Return contents from Step ❸ into the pot to be reheated. Add salt and pepper to taste.

Ingredients

Nsunabā (Swiss Chard)

The Nsunabā, or also known as a Swiss chard, is known to be rich in Calcium, Iron and Dietary Fiber.

The Nsunabā plant has large leaves, so to make washing it easier, cut them apart from the stems first.

HEALTHY COLUMN

To make vegetables rich with fiber easier to eat, blend the entire vegetable (leaves, too) in a blender.

Protect your beauty by eating healthy.

SPRING SOUP RECIPE
【春スープレシピ】

Okinawan Carrot Soup with Brown Rice

⏱ Cooking time 20minutes 【77kcal / Per serving】
(※Cooling time not included.)

kae's voice

Spices such as Cardamom and Cumin seeds make all the difference in the scent and flavor of a recipe. Cardamom possesses a superior aroma and is also at times called the "Queen of Spices". It is one of my favorite.

Ingredients(Yield: 4 servings)

Okinawan carrot	carrot (100g)
Onion	1/2 onion
Garlic	1 clove
Ⓐ Chicken consommé	1 cube
Water	500cc
Brown rice	60g
Salt	Pinch of salt
Cardamom	to preferred taste
Cumin seed	to preferred taste
Salt	to preferred taste
Pepper	to preferred taste
Olive oil	1 tablespoon

Directions

❶ Slice the Okinawan carrot and onion, then mince garlic clove.

❷ Place onions and pour olive oil in the pot prior to turning on heat. Once you can smell the mixture cooking, add the Okinawan carrots and onions then sauté.

❸ Add the pre-made mixture Ⓐ to the ingredients prepared in Step 2 and heat to boil. Once it begins to boil, cover the pot and allow it to simmer on low heat for 10 minutes. Turn off heat once it has simmered and allow it to cool. Once cooled, place mixture in a blender to be mixed.

❹ Return mixture to pot to warm and add salt to preferred taste. Sprinkle pepper to preferred taste, too.

Ingredients

Okinawan carrots

Okinawan Carrots are rich in beta-Carotene and nutrition from it can be best absorbed by cooking it with oil.

Garlic often burns quickly so remember to place it with the olive oil in the pot prior to turning on the heat.

When you blend ingredients in a blender, make sure you blend it until it has smooth texture.

HEALTHY COLUMN

Spices and herbs deepen the flavor of a dish. It can also help reduce the amount of salt in a recipe, so I would hope everybody becomes wise in how they can be used.

Decorate your life
and yourself with a flower.

SPRING SOUP RECIPE

Spring Cabbage and Okinawan Leek Pottage

Cooking Time 30minutes 【118kcal / Per Serving】

kae's voice

To recognize the distinct umami of an ingredient, eat it when it is in season.
To know the actual flavor of an ingredient, you must taste it during its season.

Ingredients (Yield: 4 servings)

Spring cabbage .... 3 leaves (130g)
Okinawan leek 50g
Chinese yam 3cm
Garlic 1clove
Water........................ 350cc
Sault .... 1/2 teaspoon
White pepper .... to preferred taste
Olive oil .... 1 teaspoon Decorations
【Decorations】
Cabbage .... to preferred taste
Edible flower .... to preferred taste

Directions

1. Cut spring cabbage leaves into 2-3 cm pieces and chop Okinawan leeks. Cut Chinese yam into 1 cm blocks and mince garlic into 1-2 mm sizes.
2. Pour the olive oil and place garlic into a pot prior to turning on the heat. Once you can smell the mixture cooking, add Okinawan leeks and sauté until they are soft. Add remaining ingredients and continue to sauté. Add water and heat to boil. Once it begins to boil, cover the pot and allow it to simmer on low heat for 10 to 15 minutes.
3. Allow the mixture made in Step 2 to cool, and then blend them in the blender. Return mixture to pot to warm and add salt to preferred taste.
4. Pour soup into a bowl, add pepper to preferred taste, and then decorate with a cabbage leaf and edible flower.

Ingredients

Okinawan leek

Okinawan Leeks helps to increase your metabolism and recover from exhaustion and fatigue. Spring Cabbage has a soft and sweet flavor and also is rich in Vitamin C and Dietary Fiber.

Okinawan leek should be sautéed until they are soft.

HEALTHY COLUMN

Take advantage of ingredients that are sticky to thicken the texture of your recipe. To know the features of an ingredient can help in increasing the nutritious value while lowering the calorie intake.

Fresh Sweet Corn Pottage

⏲ Cooking time: 20_minutes 【182kcal (Dairy milk)・156kcal (Soy milk)・117kcal (Almond milk / Per serving) (*Cooling time not included.)

kae's voice | When finding yourself saying, "Wow, I'm tired", add a few "sweet" vegetables to your recipe.The slight sweetness of the ingredients will help to relieve some of that stress off your shoulders.

Embrace your body and soul with warmth.

SPRING SOUP RECIPE

Ingredients (Yield: 4 servings)

Sweet corn .... 1 ear
A:
  Onion .... 1/2 onion
  Okinawan carrot ... 1/2 Okinawan carrot
Garlic .... 1 clove
Salt .... to preferred taste
Pepper .... to preferred taste
Olive oil .... 2 teaspoons

B:
  Chicken consommé 1 cube
  Dairy milk 500cc
  Rice 30g
  Cardamom powder 1/2 teaspoon
  Cumin powder ... 1/2 teaspoon

Ingredients

Sweet corn

To choose the best ear of corn, make sure you choose one that still is in its husk and has the brightest and plumpest kernels. If the husk is already removed, choose the one with the softest kernels.

Directions

1. Remove kernels while leaving some for decorative use.
2. Cut all ingredients in the pre-made mixture **A** into julienne strips. Mince garlic.
3. Pour the olive oil and place garlic into a pot prior heating. Once mixture cooks, add pre-made mixture **A** and sauté.
4. Add Pre-made mixture **B** to the mixture in Step **3** and kernels from Step **1**. Heat to boil. Once it begins to boil, cover the pot and simmer on low heat for 10 minutes.
5. Allow the mixture in Step **4** to cool, blend in the blender. Puree mixture with fine strainer, return to pot to reheat. Add salt and pepper to preferred taste.
6. Pour soup into a bowl and decorate the kernels.

Place the ear of the corn vertically and hold it firmly to avoid it from rolling around and to cut kernels as large as possible.

HEALTHY COLUMN

Sweet corns possess the highest amount of calories in comparison to other vegetables, but it is rich in Vitamin B1, B2 and E. Rice is used to substitute flour (or other dry ingredients) and butter to make the soup thicker and recipe healthier.

Taste the soup flow smoothly down your throat while your body absorbs the delicious flavor.

Asa Soup

Cooking Time 10minutes 【33kcal / Per serving】

kae's voice: Spring is here! The sight of Asa (sea lettuce, kelp) brings warmth to my heart. The combination of finely-grated Togan (winter melon) and fluff beaten eggs are a perfect match with the Asa.

SPRING SOUP RECIPE

Ingredients

Asā (Fine Kelp)

Asa is rich in Dietary Fibers, Calcium, Vitamin A and Folic Acids. It is an ingredient which is most caring and kind to women.

Ingredients (Yield: 4 servings)

Dry Asa (sea lettuce, kelp) ··· 2g
Togan (winter melon) ······ 100g
Eggs (beaten) ············ 1 egg
A ⎡ Water················· 500cc
⎣ Chicken soup stock··· 1 tablespoon
   Soy sauce ··········· 1/2 teaspoon
B ⎡ Starch ·············· 1/2 tablespoon
⎣ Water················· 1/2 tablespoon
Salt ························ to preferred taste
Pepper ···················· to preferred taste
Sesame oil ··············· 1/2 teaspoon

HEALTHY COLUMN

Although the size of the winter melon predicts the degree of taste, flavor, and amount of juices it has, often times pure serving size can be too much for people. We suggest fine grating the entire thing and preserving it by placing it in the freezer (refer to the pictures below for examples).

Directions

❶ Soak the Asa in water until it is has a soft texture. Finely grate the winter melon.

❷ Combine the pre-made mixture **A** and the winter melon in a pot and turn on heat. Heat till it boils and skim foam off of the mixture. Add watered starch to thicken.

❸ Drizzle the fluffed eggs into mixture made in Step ❷ by pouring it in a circular motion making sure the egg does not lump up. Once the egg rises to the surface, turn off the heat and add salt and pepper to preferred taste.

❹ Add Asa and preferred amount of sesame oil for scent.

Place the Togan so that it may be secured firmly and remove the skin.

Firmly hold the Togan diagonally and grate.

Pour Togan evenly in an ice tray.

Aim to be one with beautiful shining skin.

SPRING SOUP RECIPE

Cream of Paprika

⏲ Cooking Time 35 minutes (※Cooling time not included.)
【160kcal (Dairy milk)・152kcal (Soy Milk)・141kcal (Almond Milk) / Per serving】

kae's voice | To look and feel your best, be consciousness of your goal and make the effort to supplement what nutrients you may be missing in your daily diet. Just a reminder, that what you eat has an everlasting impact on your life.

Ingredients (Yield: 4 servings)

Paprika	1 paprika (160g)
Ginger	1 root
Butter	25g
ⓐ Dairy milk	150cc
ⓐ Chicken Consommé	1 cube
ⓐ Water	350cc
Salt	to preferred taste
Pepper	to preferred taste

【Decorations】

Fresh cream	50cc
Nuts (Mince)	to preferred taste
Color peppers	to preferred taste
Black pepper	to preferred taste

Directions

❶ Chop paprika. Peel and slice ginger.

❷ Place butter and paprika in a pot prior to turning on the heat. While being careful not to burn the ingredients, cook for 10 minutes.

❸ Combine pre-made mixture ⓐ and sliced ginger to the ingredients in Step ❷. Set to low heat, cover the pot and allow to simmer for 10 minutes.

❹ Allow the mixture made in Step ❸ to cool, and then blend them in the blender. Puree mixture with fine strainer or sieve, and then return it to pot to warm. Add salt and pepper to preferred taste.

❺ Pour mixture from Step ❹ into a bowl and decorate with foamed cream nuts. Add grounded black peppers to preferred taste.

Ingredients

Paprika

Paprikas are rich in Vitamin C (especially the orange and red ones).
In addition, it contains other nutrients such as Carotene and Polyphenol.

Add to pre-made mixture ⓐ the consommé, water and ginger.

First randomly chop then, mince.

HEALTHY COLUMN

Be mindful of not using too much oil and combine it with antioxidant ingredients. Adding ingredients which are high in dietary fiber is a great idea, too. Eat healthy by always being conscious of the combination between ingredients.

Muji Soup

⏱ **Cooking Time 35minutes 【139kcal / Per serving】**
(※Boiling time for the pork ribs are not included.)

kae's voice | To me, the smell of Okinawan mountain yams and Muji are nostalgic of Okinawan foods. Their scent brings a smile to my face. Enjoy foods in their best season by not missing when they are shipped to your local supermarket.

Flavors which make you want to pass on generation to generation.

36

SPRING SOUP RECIPE

Ingredients (Yield: 4 servings)

Ta Muji (Stalk of Okinawan Mountain Yam)	250g (1/2 bundle)
Pork ribs	60g
Shima Dofu (Okinawan Tofu)	1/8 block of Shima Dōfu (125g)
Pork · Bonito broth	1 cup each
White Miso	50~60g

Directions

1. Cut the Muji along the fibers into 3~4 cm sizes. Soak in water to remove foam, and then boil. Boil pork ribs and slice in thick rectangular blocks.
2. Break apart Okinawan Tofu by hand into bite size chunks. Heat pork and bonito broth to boil, add pork ribs and Muji.
3. When mixture begins to boil add tofu and white miso (miso should be dissolved separately with broth). Stir mixture together.

Ingredients

Ta Muji (Stalk of Okinawan Mountain Yam)

Ta Muji is rich in Calcium, Potassium, and Dietary fiber. The stalk may cause an allergic reaction if you touch it with your bare hands so don't forget to use gloves when handling and preparing it.

Boil Ta Muji.

By breaking apart the tofu by hand increases the surface area where flavors can seep into easier.

HEALTHY COLUMN

This is a thick miso tasting soup, so there is less amount of broth added to it.
Don't forget to remove any excess pork fat.

A recipe full of Umami.
Recharge your body with this nutritious soup.

SPRING SOUP RECIPE

Cream of Soy with Tofu
Soy Milk Soup with Tofu 【247kcal / Per serving】

kae's voice | Okinawan tofu is made by grinding, compacting, pressing, and draining soybeans of any water. Shima Dofu (Okinawan Tofu) is the most famous traditional Okinawan foods.

Ingredients (Yield: 4 servings)

Pork back ribs	150g
Shima Dofu (Okinawan tofu)	1/8 block of Shima Dōfu (125g)
Okinawan carrot	1/4 carrot (30g)
Togan (Winter melon) or Japanese radish (daikon)	50g
Long onion	1/2 of long onions (40g)
Seasonal green leaf vegetable	1/4 bunch
Ginger slice	2 slices
Shiokonbu (Salted seaweed/kelp)	1/2 tablespoon
White miso	40g
Water	300cc
Soy milk	300cc

Ingredients

Shima Dofu (Okinawan Tofu)

Shima Dofu has less moisture in comparison to tofu made on mainland Japan. This increases the amount of calories and fat in the tofu, so be mindful of how much you eat.

Directions

1. Cut all ingredients into bite-sizes.
2. Combine water and white miso in a pot, and then heat to boil. Add pork back ribs, Okinawan carrots, and winter melon. Cook till ingredients are tender.
3. Add remaining ingredients to the mixture made in Step 2. Add soy milk and turn off heat slightly before it begins to boil.

Cut Okinawan carrots into bite-sizes.

Soy milk will easily curdle if it is heated too long or on too high of heat. Remember to turn off the heat right before it begins to boil.

HEALTHY COLUMN

Proteins and oils in vegetable are a vital part of your health. They are healthy ingredients which are high in Vitamins B1 and B2, Calcium, and Iron.

"Soup"-The Secret All-Around Ingredient

The amount of nutrients for cream-based soups can be increased by substituting "Dairy Milk" with "Almond Milk".

"Soup"-The Secret All-Around Ingredient

200ml
134kcal

Dairy Milk

Dairy milk is rich in calcium. It actually has 8 times more calcium than soy milk. In additions, it has well balanced amount of nine different amino acids and 8 times more vitamin B2 than soy milk.

200ml
92kcal

Soy Milk (no preservatives or added ingredients)

Soy milk is rich in Soy isoflavones, vitamin E, and iron. It is low in calories and has no cholesterol. The Soy isoflavones helps to regulate hormones in women and is claimed to help lighten symptoms caused by menopause and osteoporosis.

200ml
30kcal

Almond Milk (no sugar)

Almond milk is said to be the best source of nutrients amongst all supplementary foods. It is low in calories and rich in vitamin E. Vitamin E consists of an acidic chemical which is claimed to have an anti-aging effect on the body. It also consists of insoluble dietary fibers which help to maintain a healthy digestive system.

Each of the three types of milks is terrific for your body in their own way. Please pick-and-choose the milk that best suits what your body tells you it needs.

Making your recipe creamier or thicker using the starch in Rice and Potatoes

Substitute flour with rice or brown rice (unprocessed) to give your soup that extra thickness while keeping it easy on your stomach. The same can be done with potatoes (best when used in season) and to add a little extra vitamin C for your skin.

My Favorite Spices

Cummins
A unique aroma with a bitter yet spicy flavor. Goes well with bitter vegetables, soups, and other ingredients with a sharp flavor. Cumin seeds refer to the seeds of the flower.

Coriander
A citrusy sweet aroma softens the sharp smells of ingredients. Enhances the umami flavor and goes well with meats, sea foods, and soup dishes.

Cinnamon
This spice possesses an aroma exclusive to it and a sweet yet, slightly spicy taste. It is often used to add fragrance to various deserts, snacks, and drinks.

Cardamom
One of the oldest spices in the world which has a soothing aroma. Often used in curry, sauces, dressings and cakes. Customary in Northern Europe and India to chew Cardamom Wholes after meals.

Chinese Five-Spice Powder
Representative of Chinese spices and has an exotic yet, sweet aroma. Mix of cloves, cinnamon, fennel, sansho Japanese pepper, chenpi, and more. Used to add authentic Chinese flavor and aroma to meats and other dishes.

Summer Soup Recipes
Delicious Summer soup

The marvels of Okinawa are the most apparent during this season.
People's hearts are awed during the day,
by the oceans sparkling blue and emerald green water.
However, as the evening arrives their hearts are further filled
by how the sunset transforms the water into a champagne gold.
There are many people who say they love Okinawa.
The reasons vary but do you truly need a reason
to find yourself in love with the island.
To fully experience the island, dig deeper by asking yourself
about what and why you love it so much.
For such answers and guidance, I would suggest searching
within the Summer ingredients of Okinawa.

Summer Soup Recipes

1 Okura Soup

2 Togan Soup

3 Nakami Soup

4 Chilled Peach Pottage

5 Exotic Okinawa

6 Chilled Watermelon and Kiwi Fruit Soup

7 Asian Flavored Sparassis (Cauliflower Mushroom) Soup

Eat foods high in fiber first.

SUMMER SOUP RECIPE

Okura Soup

⏲ Cooking Time 10 minutes 【20kcal / Per Serving】

kae's voice | This soup is for times when you had too much to eat or nonstop feasts with friends. I suggest that it may be a good idea to make it a habit of helping your body reset from such times.

Ingredients (Yield: 4 servings)

Okura (a little salted)	5~6 okura
Enoki mushroom	1/2 bags of enoki
Mozuku (Mozuku seaweed)	40g
Water	500cc
Chicken consommé	1 cube
Salt・Pepper	to preferred taste
Soy sauce	1/2 teaspoon
Japanese Sake	1 tablespoon

Ingredients

Mozuku (Mozuku seaweed)

The source of the slimy texture of the seaweed is Fucoidan, a chemical which is often seen in other types of seaweed. Studies have shown it can help protect and improve the body from daily things which puts stress on it.

Directions

❶ Use salt to remove the fuzz from the Okura by simultaneously rolling and lightly pressing it on a cutting board. Slice okra into ring pieces. Chop Enoki mushrooms into 1cm thick pieces.

❷ Wash mozuku seaweed prior to chopping it.

❸ Combine water, consommé and ingredients from Step ❶ in the pot, and then turn on heat to a temperature where all ingredients can be cooked. Add seasonings to preferred taste.

❹ Add mozuku seaweed.

Place Okra horizontally on the cutting board, and then use salt to remove the fuzz from the Okura by simultaneously rolling and lightly pressing it with the palms of your hand.

After the fuzz has been removed, trim the edges surrounding the area which connects the stem to the main body of the okra.

HEALTHY COLUMN

Slimy textured ingredients can clean and maintain our good health. It is also said that it supports healthy bowel movement and regulates the level of insulin in the blood.

I am always here for you.
From: The Elephant

SUMMER SOUP RECIPE

Togan soup

🕐 Cooking Time 40 minutes 【60kcal / Per serving】

kae's voice | Can you taste the distinct flavor and umami each ingredient has? Don't miss the opportunity to know that each ingredients has a unique "harmonizing" flavor, aroma, and umami that goes with it.

Ingredients (Yield: 4 servings)

Togan (Winter melon)	300g
Peeled shrimp (a little salt and starch)	8 shrimps
Shimeji mushroom	1/3 package
ⒶJapanese leek	3 cm (7g)
Ginger	1 root
Dry shrimp (Soak in water)	10g
ⒷChicken stock	1 teaspoon
Water	500cc
Japanese Sake	1 teaspoon
Salt	1 teaspoon
Sesame oil	1 teaspoon
Starch	2 teaspoon
Water	2 teaspoon

【Decorations】
Japanese Leeks (Minced) ……… to preferred taste

Directions

❶ Cut Togan into bite-sizes and devein the shrimp. Rinse shrimp with watered down starch to remove (smell). Tear shimeji mushroom by hand.

❷ Ingredients in pre-made mixture Ⓐ should be minced.

❸ Heat sesame oil in a pot and sauté pre-made mixture Ⓐ Once you can smell the mixture cooking, add ingredients from Step 1. Add pre-made mixture Ⓑ, and then heat till boil while remove excess foam from the surface. Cover pot and allow it to simmer for 15 minutes. Add watered down starch to mixture for thickness. Pour into bowl and sprinkle Japanese leeks.

Ingredients

Togan (Winter Melon)
The moist and soft meat of the Winter Melon allows it to travel smoothly down your throat. It is rich in water and Cilium which is perfect for those hot seasons where you find yourself precipitating a lot.

To devein the shrimp, make a slit into the back of it, use a toothpick to hook and remove it.

Tear shimeji mushroom by hand into bite-sizes.

HEALTHY COLUMN

Try using various aromatic vegetables which help add a secret flavor to the dish. They are a great source for adding softness and depth to your recipe. It helps to eliminate excess use of salt and sugar, too.

Only time and hard work can describe the true meaning of "omotenashi" (actions of courtesy and thoughtfulness)

Nakami Soup

Cooking Time 80 minutes 【121kcal / Per serving】

kae's voice
A traditional and representative dish of Okinawa. The time and hard work to prepare and cook is absolutely worth the taste! I hope to pass on the tradition to others by cooking it properly and not taking short cuts.

SUMMER SOUP RECIPE

Ingredients (Yield: 4 servings)

Nakami (Pork Organs) (large/small intestine and stomach)	240g
Flour	to preferred taste
Oil	4 tablespoons
Water	to preferred taste
Dry mushroom	2~3 slices
Pork stock and salmon stock	250cc each
Salt	more than 1 teaspoon but less than 2 teaspoons
Soy sauce	to preferred taste
Hihachi (Okinawan black pepper) or grounded ginger	to preferred taste

Ingredients

Nakami (Pork Organs)

Nakami is rich in various Vitamins, Zinc and Iron. It is also so rich that it may raise your cholesterol level so be mindful of how much you enjoy it.

Directions

1. Soak pork organs in water, and then repeat washing them in flour and water 2-3 times. Pork should be washed until the surface is smooth. Cut pork into 5~6 cm by 8mm~1cm rectangular pieces.
2. Heat oil in the pot, add ingredients from Step 1 and sauté. Wash pork with hot water.
3. In a separate pot, heat water to boil and then add ingredients from Step ❷. Continue to cook and remove fat from surface until the pork is tender enough to tear by hand.
4. Soak mushroom in water, and cut them to the same length as pork.
5. Combine broth and heat to boil. Combine ingredients from Step ❸ (pork only) and 4 to broth. Add salt and soy sauce, and then simmer on low heat for 10 minutes. Allow flavor to soak into ingredients.
6. Pour Nakami soup in bowl and decorate with Okinawan black pepper or ground ginger.

HEALTHY COLUMN

Before cooking, the first step is to thoroughly wash the pork meat. "Precision" is a key step in preparing this dish properly, Another step is to sauté it in oil and wash with hot water. This is a recipe you can surely experience the true meaning of "proper preparation".

To remove the pungent smell of the pork, soak it in water then, repeatedly rub and wash with flour and water.

Make sure to thoroughly wash the outside and inside of the pork.

Look for how the cells in your body begin to shine.

SUMMER SOUP RECIPE

Chilled Peach Pottage

Cooking Time 10minutes
【110kcal (Dairy milk) ・106kcal (Soy Milk) ・99kcal (Almond Milk) / Per serving】

kae's voice
I thought up this recipe when I was pondering over how we can make our skin beautiful.Why not enjoy this dish at a brunch on your day off? I hope everybody has another wonderful day.

Ingredients (Yield: 4 servings)

A
- Dragon fruits (Red) ········ 100g
- Paprika (Red) ············· 1/8paprika (20g)
- Onion ····················· 1/8onion (25g)

B
- Your favorite herbs ······ to preferred taste
- Ground garlic ············ 1/2teaspoon
- Rice ····················· 30g
- Almond milk ·············· 75~80cc
- Salt ····················· A pinch of salt

Olive oil ·················· 1 teaspoon
Wine vinegar ··············· 1/2tablespoon
Salt ······················· to preferred taste

【Decorations】
Dry fruits (Orange slice) ··· 4slices
Whip cream·················· to preferred taste
Grain pepper ··············· to preferred taste

Directions

❶ Chop pre-made mixture **A** into small random size pieces.

❷ Combine pre-made mixture **B** and ingredients from Step ❶ in a blender and blend.

❸ Add olive oil and wine vinegar and blend again. Periodically check flavor and add salt to preferred taste.
Cool in refrigerator for 2~3 hours.

❹ Pour ingredients from Step ❸ in bowl, and decorate with fruits dry fruits, lightly foamed cream, and grinded pepper.

Ingredients

Dragon Fruits

The Dragon Fruit is one of the most captivating fruits amongst all tropical fruits. It is rich in Potassium, Magnesium, Polyphenols, Dietary Fibers, and Vitamin B.

Add rice to thicken soup.

Add a pinch of salt. In Japan, a "pinch of salt" refers to the amount of a dry ingredient you can pick up using only your thumb, pointer finger, and middle finger.

HEALTHY COLUMN

I wanted to create a recipe that would help improve a person's health, beauty, and life energy. As a result, I combined the nutrition found in the dragon fruit, paprikas (both are rich in Polyphenol), and onions (which is rich in Ally Sulfide) into this one dish.

A Smile from Okinawa and Asia

SUMMER SOUP RECIPE

Exotic Okinawa

summer soup 13

🕐 Cooking Time 70 minutes 【141kcal /Per serving】
(❊Overnight Settling time not included.)

kae's voice | Both Okinawan food and Asian herbs possess a unique flavor and aroma that I love! Cooking shares the same steps of how we must be mindful of each other's uniqueness.

Ingredients (Yield: 4 servings)

Pork	280g
Goya (Okinawan bitter melon)	1/2 of Gōya (100 g)
Togan (Winter melon)	180g
Tomato	1/2 tomato
Okura or Urizun beans (winged beans)	4 beans
Water	750cc
Ⓐ Japanese Sake	1 tablespoon
Ⓐ Salt	1 teaspoon
Ⓐ Lemon grass	to preferred taste
Mini-tomatoes	8 mini-tomatoes
Squeezed Shiuwasa Juice (Okinawan bitter lemon)	2 Shikuwasa worth of juice

Directions

❶ Remove seeds from both melons and cut into bite-sizes. Chop tomatoes and cut winged beans into bite-sizes.

❷ Combine pork and given amount of water in pot. Heat to boil. Remove excess fat by skimming surface while it boils. Add pre-made mixture Ⓐ and Goya into pot and allow it to simmer on low heat for 30 minutes. Add winter melon and tomatoes, and then to allow it to simmer on low heat for another 30 minutes. Turn off heat and allow it to cool. Next, refer to "Secret Fat Removing Techniques".

❸ Take pork from Step ❷, cut into bite-sizes and return to pot, and then begin reheating mixture. Add winged beans and mini-tomatoes and heat till boil. Once boiling, then turn off heat and stir in Okinawan bitter lemon juice. Remove lemon grass and pour into bowl.

Ingredients

Goya (Okinawan Bitter Melon)

Contains a type of Vitamin C which does not easily break down with heat and tastes great when cooked with oils. The bitterness helps to strengthen the digestive system and stimulate your appetite. Take advantage of such features to help you through hot summers.

Firmly hold one half of the Goya and remove the batting in the middle by scooping it with a spoon.

Cut Shikuwasa in half and squeeze juices in pot.

HEALTHY COLUMN

Always cook the Goya first! Often times, recipes ask that the pork is boiled first and remove the fat but instead, you can make the dish healthier by simply combining all the ingredients and spices together to cook, and then allow it to sit overnight in the refrigerator. This is my idea of eating healthier.

53

Be spontaneous and unafraid of things which may appear "different".

SUMMER SOUP RECIPE

Chilled Watermelon and Kiwi Fruit Soup

Cooking Time 10 minutes 【56kcal / Per Serving】

kae's voice | Don't you ever find yourself doing the same thing every day? When you do, try to be spontaneous and do something you might feel a little uncomfortable or different. You might end up discovering something new.

Ingredients (Yield: 4 servings)

A
- Kiwi Fruits .... 2 kiwi fruits
- Can of pineapple .... 1 slice
- Pineapple syrup .... 2 tablespoons~
- Watermelon 100g
- Water .... 1/4 cup

【Decorations】
- Any seasonal citrus fruits ... 8 slices
- Kiwi fruit .... to preferred taste
- Pineapple .... to preferred taste
- Watermelon .... to preferred taste

Directions

❶ Remove skin from kiwi fruit, remove seeds from watermelon, and cut both into small random pieces. Prepare pineapple in the similar fashion. Blend the pre-made mixture **A** in a blender and cool in refrigerator.

❷ Peel and segment the citrus fruit. Decorative fruits should be cut into small pieces.

❸ Pour the cooled down ingredients from Step ❶ into the bowl and decorate with the ingredients in Step ❷ and other fruits.

Ingredients

Watermelons

Watermelons are known to be traditional Okinawan fruit. It is rich in Potassium, B Carotene, and Lycopene. It is also an effective way to relieve the built up fatigue from the summer heat.

Cut a slit in the middle of the orange to make it easier to peel the excess skin.

HEALTHY COLUMN

When you notice you have an abundance of perishable foods, remember that you can simply freeze them all. This is a useful trick for when you need to rejuvenate yourself after you've sweated a lot or to help you through those busy mornings.

Swaying quietly, slowly, and peacefully

SUMMER SOUP RECIPE

Asian Flavored Sparassis (Cauliflower Mushroom) Soup

🕒 Cooking time: 10minutes [18kcal / Per serving]

kae's voice
"Look how cute these mushrooms are!" Simply looking at them raises the level of excitement to eat them. Ingredients are just like people, sometimes how you look is as important as how you are inside.

Ingredients (Yield: 4 servings)

Sparassis (Cauliflower Mushroom)	25g
Enoki mushroom	1/4 package
Zāsai (Swollen Stem Mustard)	40g
A ⎡ Chicken consommé	1 tablespoon
⎣ Water	500cc
Shīkuwasā (Okinawan Lemon) Juice	1 tablespoon
Your favorite Asian herbs	to preferred taste

Directions

❶ Soak sparassis in water and tear into bite-sizes. Cut Enoki mushroom and Zasai into bite-sizes.

❷ Add pre-made mixture Ⓐ and ingredients from Step ❶, cook until tender, and then add Shikuwasa juice.

❸ Place Asian herbs in bowl and pour mixture from Step ❷.

Ingredients

Sparassis (Cauliflower Mushroom)

Low in calories, but rich in Dietary Fibers and Vitamin D. Also consists of a nutrient called B Glucagon which can help strengthen your immune system.

Tear the sparassis by hand into bite-sizes.

Place the coriander in the bowl before pouring in the soup to enjoy its full scent.

Top off the soup by placing a sparassis in the middle to give it a three-dimensional look!

HEALTHY COLUMN

It makes me so happy to know that there are so many kinds of mushrooms grown in Okinawa. Hurray for good flavor, scent, beauty and health!

Attractive Food, Attractive People Part 1

In Search for "The Chosen" Ingredient: Seafood Episode

When searching for ingredients, I always strive to strengthen the trust and personal relationship with growers and manufacturers by noting their name with the ingredient (e.g. These vegetables were made by so-and-so.).
In this chapter, I would like to share the various Seafood provided by Mr. Koji Maeda.

Food for thought! Did you know that Okinawa is one of the top Tuna catching prefecture? Okinawa is surrounded by beautiful coral and ocean rich in nutrients for all sea life. Consequently, its seafood is rich in nutrients just as it's vegetables. The total amount of tuna consumption is surprisingly low and contrary to how regularly seafood is eaten. Seafood consists of particular protein which differs to what is in the meats and eggs in land or mountain animals. It consists of nutrients which help to lower neutral fat and LDL cholesterol, and stimulate HDL cholesterol growth and brain activity. It is also said to help increase memory and learning in children and senior citizens.

Now that you know it is good for you, there is nothing holding you back from trying it out. Stimulate your brain and try new things. With cooking it means to try new ingredients, seasoning, and even combinations of ingredients in your recipe. The anticipation and excitement of what comes next is a terrific way to kick-start those neurons!

Eating, like life, needs to have a steady "metabolism" to see the beauty and excitement of those things which surround it. This can open the doors to those new and prosperous ideas.

I fell in love with the Uminchu (people of the ocean) because, like the ocean, their hearts are everlasting, immense, gentle, and energetic. I deeply wish more and more people become supports for our cause.

In Collaboration with Yomitan-son Joint Fishery Union
(Uminchu Shokudou)

Autumn Soup Recipes
Delicious Autumn soup

What things remind you of Autumn?
During this season in Japan, an expression
you often hear is "Autumn Appetite".
This refers to the unstoppable urge to please your appetite with the
numerous tasty foods available during this season.
Why not try pleasing your appetite with something new?
Even preparing a recipe differently by trying a new knife technique
or combining new ingredients together can help fulfill your stomach.
It's such a great chance to try out new ingredients and seasoning.
Let the excitement of the "unknown", wake up your mind, body, and soul.
In this season, there are also many ingredients that can help strengthen
your immune system for the winter. So don't forget, the basic rule
of maintaining a healthy body is to eat healthy, too.

Autumn Soup Recipes

1 Okura Soup

2 Cream of Okinawan Pumpkin

3 Okinawan Burdock Soup

4 Cream of Mushroom and Ginger

5 Cream of Malabar Spinach

6 Beni Imo (Purple Yam) and Chestnut Soup

7 Beni Imo and Okinawan Vegetable Soup

8 Kandaba Pottage

9 Japanese Whole Fish Soup

Autumn Soup

A dish full of crunchy and steaming textures that all can enjoy.

AUTUMN SOUP RECIPE

Chinnuku Pottage

⏱ Cooking Time 20 minutes 【64kcal / Per serving】

kae's voice
Lightly break up the Chinnuku to have two different the textures. Add crushed peanuts to vary the texture even more. Now you can enjoy three varying textures when you eat it! Don't forget that the texture of a recipe can add a "fun" aspect to it.

Ingredients (Yield: 4 servings)

Chinnuku (Okinawan mountain yam) ··· 300g
Ⓐ
- Japanese leek ············· 10cm (20g)
- Consommé ············· 1 cube
- Water ····················· 500cc

Salt ······························· to preferred taste
【Decorations】
Peanuts ························· to preferred taste

Directions

❶ Peel Chinnuku, cut in 1 cm thick slices, and place them in a heat-resistant container. Lightly cover with saran wrap and heat till entire ingredient is soft. Allow it to cool and then break it up with fork. Mince Japanese leek.

❷ Combine pre-combined ingredients Ⓐ into pot, and heat till boil. Add Chinnuku to mixture once it begins to boil. Cover with lid and simmer on low heat for 10 minutes. Add salt to preferred taste.

❸ Pour mixture from Step ❷ into bowl and add crushed peanuts.

Ingredients

Chinnuku (Okinawan mountain yam)

Mountains yams are rich in calium, dietary fibers, and iron, other nutrients such as Muchin which helps strengthen the digestive system.

Wrap the Chinniku with saran wrap lightly and warm-up in microwave.

Once it has cooled a little, coarsely break it up with a fork.

HEALTHY COLUMN

Try warming yourself up from within for those times when you feel tired or not feeling so motivated. By using short cuts such as simply heating ingredients up in a microwave and breaking them up can help your body soak up the warmth it needs to be reenergized.

Overflowing color and flavor to warm your heart.

HEALTHY COLUMN

Due to the high concentration of moisture in the Okinawan pumpkin, they are exceptionally good ingredient for soups. They can be made to be "extra" healthy by toasting or grilling them.

AUTUMN SOUP RECIPE

Cream of Okinawan Pumpkin

17 autumn soup

⏱ Cooking time 20minutes
【127kcal (Dairy milk) · 117kcal (Soy milk) · 78kcal (Almond milk) · Per serving】

kae's voice: Float the dry peucedanum leaves and croutons on the surface of the soup. This will give your everyday cream of pumpkin soup an extra boost!

Ingredients (Yield: 4 servings)

Okinawan pumpkin	1/6 pumpkin (180g)
Carrot	1/5 carrot (40g)
Onion	1/2 onion
Ⓐ ⎡ Rice	30g
⎢ Cumin seeds	1/2 teaspoon
⎢ Chicken consommé	1 cube
⎣ Water	200cc
Soy milk	200cc
Oil	2 teaspoons
Salt	to preferred taste

【Decoration】
Dry peucedanum crouton ··· to preferred taste

Directions

❶ Peel pumpkin, carrots, onions, and then cut into thin slices.

❷ Heat oil and cumin seeds in pot then sauté with onions. Cook till onions are light brown and add remaining vegetables and pre-combined ingredients Ⓐ. Cover and cook for 10 minutes. Add soymilk to ingredients in Step ❷.

❸ Allow to cool, blend in blender. Return to pot and warmed. Add salt to preferred taste. Pour mixture into bowl and sprinkle dry peucedanum leave croutons.

<Dry Peucedanum Leave Croutons>
Heat diced white bread in a pan. Shake pan while sprinkling olive oil and peucedanum leaves.

Ingredients

Okinawan pumpkins
Rich in B carotene, V.B1 and V.C. Find the one with the darkest overtone and is the heaviest.

How to make dry peucedanum.

Remove the leaves of the peucedanum from stems by cutting along the edges connecting each leaf together.

Dry out leaves by heating it in the microwave.

Place dry peucedanum leaves in a plastic bag, break up gently in small pieces.

Your mouth will be filled with the taste of the seasons and gifts from the earth.

AUTUMN SOUP RECIPE

Okinawan Burdock Soup

Cooking time 20minutes
【77kcal (Dairy milk) • 166kcal (Soy milk) • 150kcal (Almond milk) / Per serving】

kae's voice: Take the burdock and blend it till it is pasty. This helps to add a new taste to your recipe when you sauté or stew it. Burdock in its proper season has an indescribable tasty aroma.

Ingredients (Yield: 4 servings)

Okinawan burdock (small amount of vinegar)	1 Okinawan burdock
Potato	1 potato
Onion	1/2 of onion
Olive oil	1 tablespoon
Butter	10g
Water	1 cup
Dairy milk	1 cup
Chicken soup stock	1 tablespoon
Salt	to preferred taste
Pepper	to preferred taste
Fresh cream	2 tablespoon

【Decoration】

Grilled onions	4 slices

Directions

1. Peel burdocks, cut diagonally in thin slices, soak in water mixed with vinegar. Place in a heat-resistant container, sprinkle water, heat in microwave for 5 minutes.
2. Chop potatoes and onions.
3. Heat olive oil in pot, sauté ingredients from Step ❷ until onions are a light brown, add butter.
4. Blend 1 cup of water and ingredients from Step ❶ and ❸ together.
5. Warm in pot ingredients from Step ❹, milk, chicken broth. Add salt and pepper to preferred taste. Finish off by adding fresh cream and place grilled onion (both sides with olive oil) on top.

Ingredients

Burdocks

There are two types of Dietary fibers (i.e. water soluble and insoluble) and the burdock possesses both. It also helps regulate a healthy blood sugar level and supports digestive organs such as the stomach and intestines.

Cut burdock into bite sizes.

To remove bitterness from the burdock, boil in vinegar water while skimming foam from surface.

HEALTHY COLUMN

Improve the nutritional value of the dish while adding variety of color, form, flavor and texture with decorative toast or grilled vegetables.

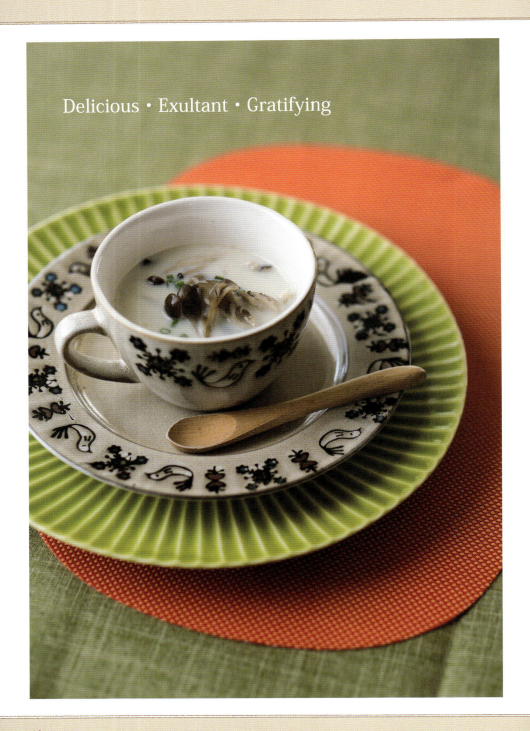

Delicious • Exultant • Gratifying

AUTUMN SOUP RECIPE

Cream of Mushroom and Ginger

Cooking Time 20minutes
【73kcal (Dairy milk) • 60kcal (Soy milk) • 41ckal (Almond milk) / Per Serving】

kae's voice

This soup is full of nutrients and umami thanks to the many different kinds of mushrooms. In Okinawa, there is an influx of many various kinds of mushrooms being produced. Please help us show our continued support for their efforts!

Ingredients (Yield: 4 servings)

Shimeji mushroom	1/3 of a pack
Maitake mushroom	1/3 of a pack
Enoki mushroom	1/3 of a pack
Kikurage mushroom	10g
Onion	1/4 onion
Ginger	1 piece
Water	250cc
Soy milk	250cc
Chicken soup stock	1 teaspoon
Salt	to preferred taste
Pepper	to preferred taste
Oil	1 teaspoon

【Decorations】

Japanese leek	preferred amount

Directions

1. Cut mushrooms into bite size portions. Soak kikurage mushrooms in water and once it is tender cut into portions of the same size. Cut onions into thin slices, mince ginger, and cut Japanese leeks into bite size portions by holding it horizontally on the cutting board.
2. Add oil, ginger, and onions in pot, then heat until scent of the ingredients being cooked can be smelled. Add mushrooms and sauté them until they are tender.
3. Add ingredients from Step A, heat however, do not let mixture boil for 2 minutes. Add salt and pepper to preferred taste.
4. Pour in bowl and place Japanese leeks.

Ingredients

Mushrooms

Each mushroom is unique in flavor and nutrients. The rich vitamins, minerals and water-soluble dietary fibers helps to build a healthy body.

Remove the mushrooms from its base and by hand, break it apart into bite size pieces.

HEALTHY COLUMN

The base of the mushroom is high in nutrition so try to only remove as little as possible. The caps of the mushroom are rich in umami, too. The maitake mushroom, shimeji mushroom and eringi mushroom can be used to add volume to your dish.

Cream of Malabar Spinach

Cooking Time 20minutes 【161kcal (Dairy milk)・135kcal (Soy milk)・96kcal (Almond milk / Per serving)】
(※Cooling time not included.)

 kae's voice: To those who find themselves not so fond of the distinctive aroma of vegetables grown in Okinawa, I highly recommend using your favorite herbs or spices to make the dish to your own taste.

AUTUMN SOUP RECIPE

Ingredients (Yield: 4 servings)

Malabar spinach	100 g
Onion	1/2 onion
Garlic	1 clove
Olive oil	1 tablespoon
Salt	to preferred taste
Pepper	to preferred taste

A
- Chicken consommé 1 cube
- Dairy milk 500cc
- Rice 60 g
- Cardamom powder to preferred taste
- Cumin powder to preferred taste

【Decoration】
Edible Chrysanthemum preferred amount

Ingredients

Malabar spinach

Rich in B carotene, calcium, magnesium, iron, and vitamin C. The greener the better! It's an all-around ingredient which your body needs!

You are what you eat.

Directions

1. Wash malabar spinach.
2. Thinly slice onions and mince garlic.
3. Combine olive oil and garlic in pot, then heat till scent of the ingredients being cooked can be smelled. Add onions and sauté till it is light brown, and then add Malabar spinach.
4. Add pre-made ingredients **A** into mixture made in Step 2. Cover with lid and allow it to simmer on low heat for 10 minutes. All content to cool then add to blender to be blended. Once blended, return mixture into pot then heat till it is warm. Add salt to preferred taste.
5. Pour mixture made in Step 4 into a bowl and lay edible Chrysanthemums onto the surface. Sprinkle pepper to preferred taste.

Sauté the malabar spinach until they are tender.

Once the mixture begins to boil, combine the rice to it.

HEALTHY COLUMN

For those people who dislike the sharp or tingly smells of certain ingredients, try parboiling, sautéing, grilling or adding heat to them before preparing them for a dish. An easy and sure way to thicken soups is to use rice.

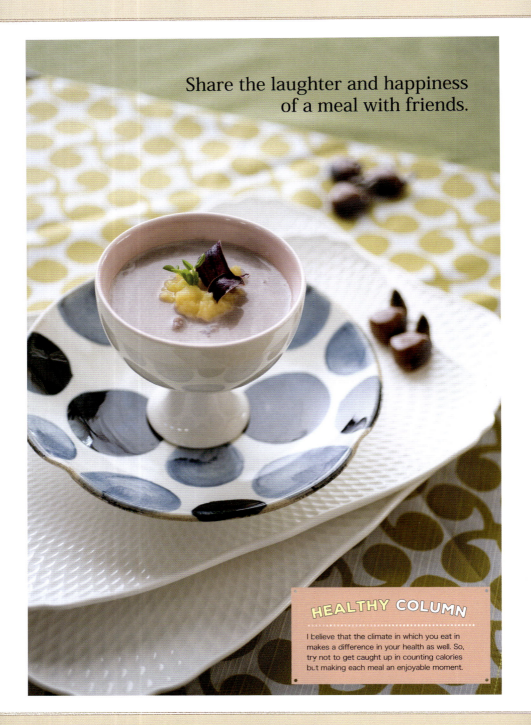

Share the laughter and happiness of a meal with friends.

HEALTHY COLUMN

I believe that the climate in which you eat in makes a difference in your health as well. So, try not to get caught up in counting calories but making each meal an enjoyable moment.

AUTUMN SOUP RECIPE

Beni Imo (Purple Yam) and Chestnut Soup

Cooking Time 35minutes
【180kcal (Dairy milk) · 161kcal (Soy milk) · 134kcal (Almond milk) / Per serving】

kae's voice: I cannot reiterate enough the value of sharing a meal with those who you love and care about. There is so much joy which can be brought by it. I hope these recipes can help make those moments even more priceless.

Ingredients (Yield: 4 servings)

Beni imo (Purple yam)	150g
Onion	1/4 onion
Butter	5g
Sugar	A pinch of sugar
Water	200cc or more
Dairy milk	300cc
Chicken consommé	1cube
Salt	to preferred taste
Pepper	to preferred taste
Peeled chestnut	50g
Water	50cc
Dairy milk	1/4 cup
Salt	to preferred taste
Pepper	to preferred taste
【Decoration】	
Fresh cream	preferred amount
Purple yam chips	to preferred taste
Sprout of pea	to preferred taste

Ingredients

Beni imo (Purple yam)

Rich in polyphenol, vitamin A & C, and calcium. Easy to store. Just wrap in newspaper and leave it away from direct sunlight

Directions

1. Peel Beni imo, chop into 1cm cubes, and soak in water. Thinly slice onion.
2. Warm butter in pot, add ingredients from Step 1, sugar, and enough water to immerse all of the yam. Heat on high till boil. Once boiling, lower heat to low and allow yams to boil until soft.
3. Blend ingredients from Step 2, milk, and chicken consommé.
4. Warm mixture from Step 3. Add salt and paper to preferred taste.
5. Heat peeled chestnuts in a separate pot for 10 minutes or until chestnuts are soft.
6. Blend ingredients in Step 5 and milk. (*)
7. Warm mixture in Step 6 in pot. Add salt and paper to preferred taste. Pour mixture from Step 4 in bowl (leave room in bowl). Pour mixture in Step 7 in the center of the bowl. Add fresh cream, purple yam and pea sprouts for decoration.
8. (*)I used a small food processing machine instead of a blender for this step.

Soaked yam in water first to remove bitterness and preserve color.

Take the time to reset from a busy day.

AUTUMN SOUP RECIPE

Beni Imo and Okinawan Vegetable Soup

⏲ Cooking Time 15minutes 【56kcal / Per serving】

kae's voice | How much "healthy" food did you eat this week? Were there any days you treated yourself too much and did allow yourself to forget those vital nutrients you need? Are you taking good care of your body?

Ingredients (Yield: 4 servings)

Beniimo (Purple yam) ············· 1 small Beniimo
Seasonal Okinawan vegetable 20 slices
Soup stock ······················· 500 cc
Salt ································ 1/2 teaspoon
Light soy sauce ················ a little less than a teaspoon

Directions

❶ Wash Beni imo (do not peel) and slice into 1 cm thick slices. Soak in water then parboil.
❷ Parboil Okinawan vegetables.
❸ Add soup stock and ingredients from Step ❶ in pot. Heat till mixture begins to boil and then add salt, light soy sauce, and oil to preferred taste.
❹ Pour ingredients from Step ❸ in bowl and decorate with Okinawan vegetables.

Ingredients

Unche
(Water spinach)

Water Spinach is rich in calcium, iron, vitamin A, B1, B2 and C. The stalk portion of the spinach can also be included in the recipe, too.

Cut purple yam (beni imo) into thick circle-slices.

Heat water to boil and lightly cook each Okinawan vegetable in hot water.

HEALTHY COLUMN

An alternative approach to help supplement the nutrients you cannot get in your daily meals is to remember that people often can stick to a plan or diet that is simple. Thus, I believe the best thing to do is to avoid over-planning or strategizing your meals.

75

"Okinawan vegetables" are Okinawa's treasure.

AUTUMN SOUP RECIPE

Kandaba Pottage

⏱ Cooking Time 20minutes (※Cooling time not included.)
【108kcal (Dairy milk)・92kcal (Soy milk)・69kcal (Almond milk) / Per serving】

kae's voice: Kandabā is the king of Okinawan vegetable in my ranking.
It is the vegetable which has enough nutrition, heath, energy and beauty.

Ingredients (Yield: 4 servings)

Kandaba	60g
Onion	1/2 onion
Ⓐ Chicken consommé	1 cube
Ⓐ Water	200cc
Ⓐ Rice	30g
Dairy milk	300cc
Salt	to preferred taste
Pepper	to preferred taste
Oil	2 teaspoons

【Decoration】

Grilled Hechima	4 slices

(Edible Luffa <Loofah> gourd plant)

Ingredients

Kandaba

Rich in vitamin A, C, B1, and B2, polyphenol, and dietary fibers. Also knowns as the climbing plant it's leaves are edible. It does wonders for your health so give it a try.

Directions

❶ Wash Kandaba leaves and remove access water from leaves. Julienne onions.

❷ Heat oil in pot, sauté onions until they are light brown. Add Kandaba leaves and lightly sauté ingredients together. Add pre-made mixture Ⓐ to pot and heat 5 minutes or until mixture begins to boil. Turn off heat, add milk, and then allow mixture to cool.

❸ Add ingredients from Step ❷ into blender to blend.

❹ Return mixture made in Step ❸ in pot and heat till warm. Add salt and paper to pre-ferred taste.

❺ Pour mixture from Step ❹ into bowl and decorate with Grilled Hechima.

Add Kandabā to onions and sauté quickly.

Peel Edible Luffa and cut in thick circular-slices or thick half moon shape-slices. Warm pan with oil prior to cooking the Luffa. Cook until both surfaces are slightly browned.

HEALTHY COLUMN

In comparison to cooking various ingredients, you are able to consume all and more kinds the nutrients by pureeing ingredients in a blender. You can also combine it with dairy milk, soy milk or almond milk for a change in flavor.

Japanese Whole Fish Soup

autumn soup 24

🕒 Cooking Time 15minutes 【398kcal / Per serving】

kae's voice | Okinawan people often do not consume a lot of seafood, although it possesses a vital yet, unique type of protein. I hope you can taste and feel the many gifts from the beautiful ocean surrounding Okinawa.

AUTUMN SOUP RECIPE

Ingredients (Yield: 4 servings)

A
- Whole white fish meat ··· 800g
- Salt ··· 1/2 teaspoon

- Water ··· 800cc
- Japanese Sake ··· to preferred taste
- Soy sauce ··· to preferred taste
- Salt ··· to preferred taste

- Green bok choy ··· 1/2 bundle
- Japanese leek ··· 3 sticks

Strengthen your mind and body

Ingredients

White fish meat

White-fish meat is a great source of high quality protein and fat. In comparison to red fish meat it has less fat and puts less strain on the digestive system.

Directions

1. Chop section of the fish with the most amounts of bones into random bite size portions. Sprinkle with salt to tenderize meat.
2. Cut green bok choy into bite size portions. Cut Japanese leeks into 4 cm lengths.
3. Combine the amount of water noted in the recipe with ingredients in Step 1 in a pot. Heat until mixture begins to boil while being conscious of skimming the foam from the surface of the mixture. Set heat on low, add Japanese sake, soy sauce, salt, and then allow it to simmer for 5 to 10 minutes.
4. Add green bok choy and Japanese leeks, and then turn off heat.

*Add Miso (Japanese bean paste) to change flavor of the soup if preferred.

Sprinkle two pinches of salt on the fish to make it firm.

Boil on low heat and remove any access fat by skimming the foam from the surface.

HEALTHY COLUMN

By boiling the entire fish, including the bones, you are able to fully extract the natural umami flavor. This process also helps to reduce the amount of salt needed for the dish.

Attractive Food, Attractive People Part 1

In Search for "The Chosen" Ingredient: Vegetable Episode

When searching for ingredients, I always strive to strengthen the trust and personal relationship with growers and manufacturers by noting their name with the ingredient (e.g. These vegetables were made by so-and-so.). In this chapter, I would like to share the various herbs and Okinawan vegetables provided by Ms. Yoko Kishimoto.

It takes a lot of time and extreme care to grow such delicious crops.

Kishimoto Farm
TEL:090-5940-8084
HP: http://kishimoto-farm.com

Kishimoto Farm

For 20 years, Kishimoto Farm has been organically growing herbs and island vegetables. They pride themselves on absence of pesticide or artificial fertilizer in its crops. Various hotels reach out to the farm to supply their kitchens. Regardless of the genre, various chefs rely and are fanatics of the farm.

Interview between Ms. Izena and Ms. Kishimoto Izena: "It has been over 10 years since we met. Back then, nobody really knew about organic foods or island vegetables."
Kishimoto: "Your right. Now, cooks can't stop making large orders for it. Things have really changed."
Izena: "Can you guarantee the safety of the food while taking extra time caring for the crops?"
Kishimoto: "Pesticides ruins the flavor and aroma of the crop. Organic is the way to go."
Izena: "I'll continue to support crop grower to help spread the word of their passion and efforts."
Kishimoto: "I am a supporter of your dream. I also want the title of "Island with the Longest-Lived People" again. Let's work to spread the word. I'll use my herbs and vegetables to reintroduce to families the joy of eating.

\ *Let's Vegetable* /
Vegetable Specialty Shops NOW OPEN!

Come and find the vegetables needed to make your recipe's taste and nutrients shine!

Happy More Market <Okinawa Herbs and Spices World>

You can find that "once in a life-time" vegetable in season.

"In 2008 I renovated a section of my father's tomato patch to open this store", says Mr. Masahiko Wada, the owner of Happy More Market. In the beginning, Mr. Wada's store only stocked a few ingredients from roughly 10 small farm owners, but once the word got around over 800 farms jumped on the opportunity to share their crops with him. To diversify the crops he only deals directly with each farm. Hence, there is no assurance the same ingredient is sold on any given day. Many regular customers come from afar to the market. There is strong culture of food safety in the market and a sense of pride has been embedded in the market of providing locally grown and fresh crops. The market's ultimate aim is to promote the herbs, spices, and other crops grown in Okinawa to the world.

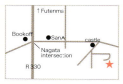

☎098-896-0657
Address／Ginowan city, Shimashi 1-247-1, Okinawa prefecture (Japan)
Hours／10:00-18:00
Closed／Sundays
Parking／Available
HP／http://www.facebook.com/happykeiko024

Thank You Farm <Organic Potato and Yam Field>

The rich Ryukyuan calcium in the soil and flowing hard water in the Ooyama District of Ginowan city, is the reason why numerous Okinawan yam (Tanmu yam) fields spread across its lands. Thank You Farm uses the natural nutrients provided in the soil with help of the microscopic organisms which live in it. They do it the "old fashion way" and avoid using any artificial fertilizers or chemicals for their crops. Mr. Yu Miyagi of the Ooyama Okinawan Yam Farmer's Union says, "The Okinawan Yam is soul food to the families in Okinawa and is irreplaceable with any other ingredient". The yam grower's pride brings about countless farmers near and afar who are in search these tasty yams.

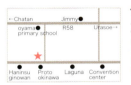

☎070-5538-8965
Address/ Ginowan city, Ooyama 5-34 Okinawa prefecture (Japan)
Parking/ Available
HP/
http://taimo39farm.te-da.net/

Paruzu <Organic Ingredients>

In Paruzu, the first thing you notice is the colorful array of vegetables on the shelves. The bright yellows, greens, and oranges are signs of freshness and season of the vegetable. The owner, Mr. Tetsu Shinoda, traveled to numerous organic farms in search of ingredients that will energize the consumer. "I make sure to meet everybody in person and speak to each of them personally. Relationships is key to building trust", says Mr. Shinoda. In addition, locally grown organic ingredients and fermented foods can be found here, too. It's a market which will surely change your outlook on what foods you want in your body.

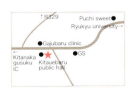

☎098-895-7746
Address/Nakagusuku, Kita Uehara 309   Hours/9:30-19:00 (Weekdays) 10:00-19:00 (Sundays/Holidays)   Closed/ 1st and 3rd Mondays of the month   Parking/ Available
HP/http://www.pals-1.com/

Winter Soup Recipes

Delicious Winter soup

The unique food culture of Okinawa was built by the countless
interactions between people and the environment they live in.
With it as a foundation, the ingredients from the ocean, land, mountains,
and the visitors to the island helped us build food legacy.
The island's sun is another reason for such blessing,
and I hope everybody can enjoy it and our foods.
I send my wishes of joy and fruitful life to all.

Winter Soup Recipes

1 Winter Okinawan Vegetable and Beef Soup

2 Spicy Yushi Dofu and Garlic Leaves Soup

3 Chopped Billfish and Vegetable Soup

4 Cream of Okinawan Carrot

5 Tender Okinawan Vegetables Soup

6 Inamu duchi

7 Cream of Chinese Cabbage and Scallops

Winter Soup

85

For those yearning for softer skin.

WINTER SOUP RECIPE

Winter Okinawan Vegetable and Beef Soup

Cooking Time 60minutes 【119 kcal / Per Serving】

kae's voice Dry skin is a concern to everyone in the winter. I suggest resolving it with foods rich in protein. Recipes which use beef tendons can be challenging, but don't worry, this one is easy!

Ingredients (Yield: 4 servings)

A
- Beef tendon ········ 200g
- Sliced ginger ········ A partial root worth

Okinawan radish ········ 180g
Okinawan carrot ········ 1/3 Okinawan carrot
Garlic leaves ············· 2 stalks
Konjac ······················ 1/4 slices
Sliced ginger ············· A partial root worth
Soup stock ················· 500cc
Sake (Japanese liquor) ········ 1 tablespoon
Miso ························· 50g
Seven flavors chili pepper to preferred taste

Directions

1. Chop beef tendons to bite size portions. Combine water, beef tendons and ginger in pot. Heat till boils while skimming the foam from the surface. Set heat on mid and simmer for 30 minutes. Drain water and set ingredients in strainer.
2. Cut radish and carrot into quarter circle slices. Cut Konjac into bite size portions and parboil.
3. Cut garlic leaves into 3 cm lengths.
4. Combine soup stock, Japanese sake, ingredients from Step ❶ and ❷, and ginger in pot, and simmer on low heat. Once the centers of the radishes are tender (check with skewer), add water-dissolved Miso, place Japanese wooden drop-lid on mixture, simmer for 15 minutes. Add garlic leaves while ingredients are simmering. Pour soup in bowl and sprinkle chili pepper powder.

○ Ingredients ○

Beef tendon

Rich in protein, low in fat, vitamin B and K, and collagen. Great source for broth to use for soups, curry, and stews.

Cut the carrot and radish into Ginkgo-leaf shape portions.

Garlic leaves should be cut into 3cm portions.

HEALTHY COLUMN Be mindful of removing any excess fat when preparing various meats. This is extra step to help build and maintain beautiful skin. By slow boiling root and leaf vegetables, ginger, and garlic leaves together you are able to create a body and heart-warming soup.

winter soup 26

Spicy Yushi Dofu and Garlic Leaves Soup

Cooking Time 20minutes 【182kcal / Per serving】

kae's voice: Keep in mind that the warmer your body is the better it moves and functions. It also has a positive side effect of keeping your spirits and mood high. So don't forget, when you feel that little chill, simply take in a warm dish.

WINTER SOUP RECIPE

○ Ingredients ○

Garlic leaves
Rich in calcium, various vitamins, iron, and Alliin. Choose ones with tender leaves and avoid storing for long periods of time.

Recipe

❶ Drain Yushi Dofu in strainer. Remove sand and other debris from clams by washing and rubbing them together.

❷ Cut Enoki mushroom and the garlic leaves in to bite size portions. Cut pork into bite size portions. Warm sesame seed oil in pot and add pork to sauté until both sides are well cooked.

❸ Combine pre-made ingredients Ⓐ, ingredients from Step ❶ and ❷ in pot and heat until clams are open. Add salt to preferred taste.

> Bring strength to others by letting your energy flow onto those around you.

Ingredients (Yield: 4 servings)

Yushi Dofu (500g of Fluffy Okinawan Tofu)	1 pack
Clams	8 clams
Enoki mushroom	1/2 packs
Garlic leaves	4 stalks
Pork	100g
Sesame oil	1 teaspoon
Ⓐ Water	400cc
Sesame oil	1 teaspoon
Gochujang (Korean hot pepper paste)	2 teaspoons
Red pepper powder	1 teaspoon
Minced Japanese leek	3 cm
Sugar	1 teaspoon
Pureed garlic	1 teaspoon
Chicken soup stock	2 teaspoons
Soy sauce	1/2 tablespoons
Japanese Sake	2 teaspoons
Salt	to preferred taste

Wash the clams and remove any debris from the surface and grooves on the outer shells by gently rubbing them together

Warm frying pan with sesame seed oil and sauté pork until excess fat is removed.

HEALTHY COLUMN

Tofu and shell fish are great source of protein. Shell fish are low in calories but high in various vital nutrients. In other word, they are an essential ingredient to support women's health.

Chopped Billfish and Vegetable Soup

⏱ Cooking Time 25minutes
【113kcal / Per serving】

kae's voice: Sake kasu (Japanese sake lees) are the leftover bits when making rice wine. It is an ingredient rich in nutrients which reminds me of the importance of tradition and ancestry.

A trendy mix of classic and modern style.

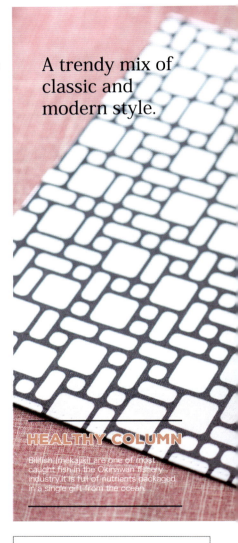

Ingredients (Yield: 4 servings)

Mekajiki (Billfish)	2 slices (70g each)
Daikon (Japanese radish)	4 cm (120g)
Okinawan carrot	1/2 carrot
Konjac	1/3 slices
Okinawan vegetable	1/4 bundle
Soup broth	450cc

Ⓐ
- Sakekasu (Japanese liquor lees) 50g
- Miso …… 1 tablespoon
- Mirin (Japanese sweet rice wine) 1 teaspoon

Directions

❶ Chop Billfish into portions slightly larger than bite size. Chop radish and Okinawan carrots into similar sizes. Use a spoon to tear bite size portions from Konjac and then boil.

❷ Cut Okinawan vegetables into 3 cm portions.

❸ Combine soup stock and ingredients from Step ❶ in pot and heat until mixture begins to boil while being conscious of skimming the foam from the surface of the mixture. Place lid and lower heat to mid.

❹ Mix together ingredients from Step ❸ with pre-made ingredients Ⓐ, add Okinawan vegetables, heat till boil, and then turn off the heat.

HEALTHY COLUMN

Billfish (mekajiki) are one of most caught fish in the Okinawan fishery industry. It is full of nutrients packaged in a single gift from the ocean.

○ Ingredients ○

Mekajiki (Billfish)
Billfish are rich in protein, DHA, vitamin D, and potassium. It is also has a great source of glutamine.

WINTER SOUP RECIPE

Cut sword fish (Mekaji) into bite size portions.

Use a spoon to tear apart the Konjac. By doing this the surface area increases thus, allowing the flavor to seep into the ingredient with ease.

WINTER SOUP RECIPE

winter soup 28

Cream of Okinawan Carrot

Cooking Time 25minutes 【96kcal / Per serving】
(※Cooling time not included.)

kae's voice: Just by warming and whipping up a small amount of milk (dairy), you are able to make your own little batch of clouds. Sometimes it is the small things that bring about those "big" smiles.

Ingredients (Yield: 4 servings)

Okinawan carrot	2/3 carrot
Onion	1/2 onion
Olive oil	1 tablespoon
ⓐ Water	300cc
ⓐ Consommé	1 package
ⓐ Oregano	1/2 teaspoon
Salt	to preferred taste
Pepper	to preferred taste
Dairy milk	to preferred taste

【Decorations】

Dry Sakuna (Dry Peucedanum Flower)	to preferred taste
Preferred Nuts	to preferred taste

Directions

❶ Thinly slice Okinawan carrots and onions.

❷ Heat olive oil in a pot, sauté ingredients from Step ❶. Once ingredients are cooked add pre-made ingredients ⓐ and heat till boil and allow to cook for 10 minutes.

❸ Allow ingredients in Step ❷ to cool then pour in blender to be blended. Return mixture to pot and heat till warm. Add salt and pepper to preferred taste.

❹ Heat milk in separate pot (do not let it boil) and use hand mixer to whip.

❺ Pour ingredients from Step ❸ in bowl and add froth from Step ❹. Decorate with Dry Sakuna and crushed nuts.

○ Ingredients ○

Okinawan carrots

Okinawan carrots are rich in B carotene and carotene. It also provides a fresh aroma and eloquent color to your dish. The leaves also have lots of nutrition so let's use the part that is soft.

Heat pot with olive oil and then, sauté Okinawan carrots and onions.

Whip milk with hand mixer.

HEALTHY COLUMN

To extract the natural sweet flavors from the carrots and onions, they should be slowly sautéed. Before you add or subtract ingredients from a recipe, think about how you can "extract" flavors from what you already have.

WINTER SOUP RECIPE

Tender Okinawan Vegetables Soup

🕒 Cooking Time 30 minutes 【117kcal / Per serving】

 | It goes without saying that you are able to maintain good health by being regularly conscious of the healthy ways you can eat an ingredient. Sometimes it is all about the level of consciousness and level of nutrition of an ingredient.

Ingredients (Yield: 4 servings)

Ginger (Minced) ············· 1 teaspoon a little over
A ┌ Okinawan carrot ··· 1/2 bundle
  │ Okinawan burdock 1/2 bundle
  │ Japanese radish ··· 100g
  │ Shimeji mushroom 1/2 package
  └ Pork ···················· 80g
Japanese Sake ············ 1 teaspoon
Soup broth ················· 700cc
Miso ························· 50g
Malabar spinach ········· 4 leaves
Oil ···························· 1 teaspoon

○ Ingredients ○

Ginger

Possesses the chemical Cineole (anti-oxidative), Ginerol, Shogaol which helps to increase body temperature and maintain healthy blood circulation. An exceptional ingredient for those in need to "warm-up" during the cold winters.

Directions

❶ Combine oil and ginger in pot and heat ingredients until scent of the ginger being cooked can be smelled. Pre-made ingredients Ⓐ should be chopped into bite sizes and sautéed in the pot with Japanese sake.

❷ Add soup stock to ingredients from Step ❶, heat until mixture begins to boil, and then place lid on pot (continue to be check mixture and skim the foam from the surface).

❸ Once ingredients in Step 2 have been well cooked, add Miso and malabar spinach.

Combine Okinawan carrots, Okinawan burdocks, Japanese radish, shimeji mushroom, pork, sake into pot and then, sauté.

The aroma of the miso can be increased by first turning off the heat then adding a dissolved portion of miso into the mixture.

HEALTHY COLUMN

Add strong herbs or spices or use Japanese sake as seasoning for accent. This cuts down on the broth or salt needed for flavor.

WINTER SOUP RECIPE

Inamu duchi

⏲ Cooking Time 80minutes 【113kcal / Per Serving】

kae's voice | The precision and delicacy in preparing this dish will make all the difference in the end. This is a culmination of Japanese culture and representative of the divine value toward "omotenashi" (i.e. hospitality). I hope you discover tranquility in the time spent in preparing it.

Ingredients (Yield: 4 servings)

Pork	60g
Dry Shiitake mushroom	2 slices
Block of Konjac	100g
Castella Kamaboko (Layered boiled fish paste)	60g
Pork and salmon broth	2 cups
White miso (Sweet taste)	40 to 60g

Directions

1. Parboil pork and slice into thin rectangular strips (tanzaku giri). Soak dry shiitake mushroom in water until it is tender, and then thinly slice. Cut Konjac similarly as pork then boil. Cut Castella Kamaboko similarly as pork and Konjac.
2. Pour broth in pot to warm. Add pork and shiitake mushroom and heat till boil. Add Konjac.
3. While boiling, add Castella Kamaboko and white miso.

◦ Ingredients ◦

Pork

Pork is rich in protein, vitamin B1 and B2, and iron. It is a vital source for key amino acids needed to help the body recover from fatigue and exhaustion.

To remove any excess fat and strong smell from pork, boil it in water first.

Cut meat into thin strips to allow the flavor to seep in with ease while improving the dishes appearance and texture.

HEALTHY COLUMN

Pork is an indispensible ingredient in recipes from Okinawa. When you use fatty sections of pork, don't forget to remove excess fat by trimming it from the meat and continuously skim the surface of foam when boiling it.

It goes without saying the glory and succulent taste of this dish.

WINTER SOUP RECIPE

Cream of Chinese Cabbage and Scallops

⏱ Cooking Time 30minutes 【70kcal / Per serving】

kae's voice
The synergy from the umami and other ingredients will descend into your stomach and then trigger the neurons in your brain to think of the only one word to respond to the taste. You will smile and utter that word,… "Delicious!"

Ingredients (Yield: 4 servings)

Ⓐ
- Chinese cabbage …… 2 slices
- Carrots …………… 1/4 carrot
- Dry shiitake mushroom 2 slices

Ginger ……………… 1 root

Ⓑ
- Can of scallops ……… 1 can
- Water……………… 200cc
- Chicken soup stock… 1/2 teaspoon

Soy milk ……………… 200cc
Salt …………………… A pinch of salt
Pepper ………………… to preferred taste
Sesame oil …………… 2 teaspoons

Directions

❶ Slice Chinese cabbages at an angle and dice carrots into 5 mm portions. Soak shiitake mushrooms in water until it is tender and julienne. Mince ginger.

❷ Combine sesame oil and ginger in pot and heat until the scent of the ginger being cooked can be smelled. Add pre-made ingredients Ⓐ and sauté.

❸ Once Chinese cabbages are tender, add pre-made ingredients Ⓑ. Heat on high till boil and place lid on pot. Lower heat to low and allow it to simmer for 10 minutes.

❹ Set heat on low and add soy milk to mixture in Step ❸. Add salt and pepper to preferred taste.

○ Ingredients ○

Chinese cabbage

Chinese cabbage is rich in calcium, potassium, and great source for taking in water. It also contains a good amount of umami, so keep that in mind when using it in your recipes.

To allow the flavor to easily seep into the Chinese cabbage, slice the stem portions at an angle to provide the largest amount of surface area.

Sauté ingredients until they are tender.

HEALTHY COLUMN

The sweetness of Chinese cabbage, the whole soup of scallops' can, the good flavor of shiitake mushroom, soy milk, sesame oil have the synergistic effect. Scallops has taurine that help us recovering from exhaustion and glycine that makes you relax.

KAE project

Established by Kae Izena, the "Collaboration of the Health Revolution and Grow Locally/Consume Locally Project" aids the aim by the Okinawan Prefectural Government of "Rejuvenation of Health and Longevity / Increased Consumption of Prefecturally Grown Ingredients".

Energize and Strengthen Okinawa with and through "Food".

Launched in April, 2016 in Yomitan City, the Kae Project's home base began in Naha. It's activities aimed to reach a wider audience and deepen its activities focus on maintaining good health. Under the advisement of individuals in the medical field, private industry, food growers and manufacturers, and consumers, it now houses six pillar projects. Together they work to revolutionize the health and food industry. It is an inclusive project with realistic solutions for all ages and fields.

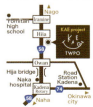

Total Wellness Project Okinawa
☎098-989-9530
Address／Yomitan village Owan 356 Synergy Square 2F,
JapanHours／10:00-18:00
Closed／Mondays
HP／http://twpo.jp/
Feel free to look us up! "Kae Project"

1. Culinary Classes

Choose from our list of classes based on your needs and goals. We offer 1) basic Japanese cooking beginner and intermediate classes, 2) classes introducing ingredients unique to Okinawa, 3) children's cooking classes and clubs, 4) cooking classes specifically designed for the working "guy", and 5) seminars and classes specific to the medical field, 6) and other special events. Come and taste our stylish and healthy recipes while experiencing the joy of cooking!

2. Raising Awareness towards Local Ingredients

We support activities which promote and market local ingredients grown on Okinawa. Activities include seminars, cooking classes, and other events which focus on using these ingredients to create new recipes and products. We aim to push forward the production of local foods for local consumption by working with the communities, city council members, prefectural government, private industries, and other organizations.

3. Fitness Classes

Motto: Cultivate a mindset toward having a healthy body through introducing educating them about stretching techniques, cardiovascular exercise, and muscular-skeletal strengthening routines. Classes held in a studio and outside. Let mother-nature help strengthen your body.

4. Health and Medical Counseling

Programs designed to help companies and organizations promote authentic ways to maintain a healthy living style to its employees. We hope in doing so helps more people stay healthy and avoid getting sick. Join us to spread the Okinawan way of staying healthy to more people.

5. Professional Development for Health and Nutrient Professionals

"A place to fulfill your intellectual appetite and polish your body and soul". Programs include; 1) lectures and seminars, 2) workshops, and 3) on-the-job training that aim to help you reflect upon yourself while deepening your understanding of Okinawa. Come and acquire a life full of knowledge and energy under the banner, "An Okinawa Full-of-Life".

6. Farm and Food Growing Education, "Team Ganju"

Established under a shared idea amongst a group of young individuals from various fields, it aims to 1) provide "hands-on" experiences and education in the farm and food growing field, 2) educate people on the food culture and traditions of Okinawa, and 3) produce events open to the public in hopes to raise the awareness towards the importance of food and its growers.

101

Student Testimonials

I chose Kae Project to learn…

- recipes that are healthy and grown locally.
- local cooking techniques with local foods.
- how to cook Okinawan recipes.
- recipes recommended by Nutritionists.
- from Ms. Kae.
- of opportunities outside of the classroom.

Our annual Christmas Party Event. It is the finale of our year.

How have you changed?

- I am more conscious of having a balanced meal.
- I need to provide more variety of ingredients for my family.
- I don't use as much oil and seasoning now.
- A good pot is important and the science in cooking.
- I enjoy cooking more!
- I feel better!
- I have more choices locally.
- I am what I eat.
- Food made up of the thoughtfulness and care towards others.
- I am more mindful of who grows my food.
- I am more conscious of the amount of salt, sugar, and fat.
- I have interest outside of that.
- I now know how to use herbs and spices in my recipes.
- I am now more cautious of table manners.
- I made great friends!

As part of our field tour program, we visited a Mozuku (sea grass) manufacturer and grower. We all clean-up the area by picking up garbage before the tour.

Student Messages to Kae Izena

It was a satisfying experience and I was able to learn something about nutrient, cooking techniques, and mannerisms. There is no other school you could feel so "at home".

The teacher's discussions were always fun. She fueled my energy.

I learned a lot about cooking, mannerisms, and vacationing.

The time was full of wonderful things. The recipes were healthy, tasty, and stylish. The time was priceless.

Her thoughts and drive had a positive impact on my life.

I loved everything about her. Anything from her personality, approach, and vitality.

The time was truly satisfying. I hope more people on Okinawa can experience what I experienced at the school.

I learned that cooking is about being mindful and grateful towards others. That includes the growers and the island of Okinawa.

I found many hints that can help during everyday cooking.

Although I am from the mainland, I feel those vegetables grow on Okinawa more dear to me now that I know how to use and prepare them.

Our meetings always reenergized me.

I like the way you could be silly.

Your classes helped revitalize my life all the times.

I grew to be more positive toward what you eat every day. To me it was a time to learn and heal. Thank you very much.

103

STAFF

【Recipes】 Kae Izena
【Director and Design】 Yuya Makishi Chizuru Maeda
【Photopraphs】 Chotaro Owan
【Styling】 office RHIZOME
【Writers】 Rie Fukumoto, Hiroshi Nakayama
【Assistant】 Ayako Tamayose, Kaori Uehara, Kazuto Kikuchi
【Chief Translator】 Todd R. Arao
【Assistant Translator】 Sarah T. Arao

【Special Thanks】
Rika Arakaki, Yuuko Ijyu, Chisato Ooshiro, Miyuki Kamiyama, Kanako Taira, Aika Nagamine
Chisaki Nashiro, Satoko Yoshida

Thank you everybody for all of the support, cooperation, and encouraging words.
I am extremely grateful for the heartwarming response by so many people.
I wish everyone, a life full of smiles and happiness.
Kae Izena

Kae Izena's Okinawa Soup Recipe Book

Print Date: Jan 14, 2018 1st Edition
Author╱ Kae Izena
Product Director╱ Takashi Oshiro
Publisher╱Editing studio Toyo Plan
Address╱4-21-5, Nishizaki Town Itoman City Okinawa Prefecture, Japan Postal Code 901-0306
TEL╱098-995-4444 FAX╱098-995-4448()
【URL】https://toyo-plan.co.jp/
Production Compositor╱Toyo Plan Printed Inc.
Manufacturer╱Okinawa Binding Inc.

※Follow international dialing procedures to call from outside Japan

All Rights Reserved. ©2017 Toyo Plan Printed in Japan
No part of this work covered by the copyright herein may be reproduced, transmitted, stored,
or used in any form or by any means graphic, electronic, or mechanical, including
but not limited to photocopying, recording, scanning, digitizing, taping, web distribution, information networks,
or information storage and retrieval systems, except as permitted by the prior written permission of the publisher.